The map is not the territory

ALFRED KORZYBSKI

MAP, ASWAN 1985

EGYPTIAN TIME

PHOTOGRAPHS BY

ROBERT LYONS

SHORT STORY BY

NAGUIB MAHFOUZ

TRANSLATED BY PETER THEROUX

INTRODUCTION BY

CHARLIE PYE-SMITH

DOUBLEDAY

NEW YORK LONDON TORONTO SYDNEY AUCKLAND

To my parents, Celia and Melvin Lyons

Published by Doubleday
a division of Bantam Doubleday Dell Publishing Group, Inc.
666 Fifth Avenue, New York, New York 10103

DOUBLEDAY and the portrayal of an anchor with a dolphin are trademarks of Doubleday
a division of Bantam Doubleday Dell Publishing Group, Inc.

Library of Congress Cataloging-in-Publication Data
Lyons, Robert.
Egyptian Time / photographs by Robert Lyons; short story by Naguib Mahfouz.
     p.   cm.
     Includes translation of: al-Mahd.
      1. Egypt—Description and travel—1981—Views.   I. Mahfūz,
Najib, 1912— Mahd. 1992. English. II. Title.
DT47.L96   1992
779' .9962055092—dc20   91-36729
                                      CIP

ISBN 0-385-42104-4
Copyright © 1992 by Robert Lyons
Photographs copyright © 1992 by Robert Lyons
Introduction copyright © 1992 by Charlie Pye-Smith
"The Cradle" copyright © 1990 by Naguib Mahfouz
"The Cradle" was originally published in Arabic in 1990, under the title "al-Mahd."
This story is published by arrangement with the American University in Cairo Press
English translation copyright © 1992 by Peter Theroux

Design by Katy Homans

All Rights Reserved
Printed in Hong Kong
October 1992
First Edition

INTRODUCTION

CHARLIE PYE-SMITH

This is a book of exceptional beauty and originality. Robert Lyons's photographs of Egypt haunt the imagination, and they find the perfect complement in "The Cradle," a story of childhood by the novelist Naguib Mahfouz. Seldom has a photographer captured so vividly and accurately the true character of Egypt and its people as Lyons has here. His approach is subtle and allusive: he tends to celebrate the commonplace rather than the spectacular, and in doing so he offers us a refreshingly honest appraisal of this quixotic country. This is not a book to be rushed: the pages which follow paint a picture of a world too rich and beguiling to be devoured in a single sitting.

One should begin, perhaps, with Mahfouz's sensuous evocation of an Egyptian childhood. The power of the story stems from its universality, for childhood "bears witness to eternal questions, to love, sex, friendship, honor, life, death, the glorious Presence of the Almighty, basic themes that develop and diversify with life"; but the childhood described by Mahfouz is also set firmly within the confines of an Egyptian city and Muslim society. Here are the streets of Cairo chock-full with peddlers, beggars and donkeys; here are the flat rooftops with their promiscuous gathering of rabbits, pigeons and poultry; and here is the neighborhood cafe with its games of backgammon, its gossip and smoking hookahs.

Mahfouz's Egypt is comradely, boisterous, sometimes chaotic; whereas the world which Lyons reveals is serene, contemplative and at times filled with a preternatural silence. The novelist and photographer have approached the country from different viewpoints: Mahfouz from that of a Cairene child; Lyons as an artist with a fresh canvas, his road to discovery untrammeled by considerations of kinship or childhood familiarity. However, both, in their separate ways, encourage us to marvel at one of Egypt's most alluring—and elusive—qualities: despite all the problems of poverty, overcrowding, regional and religious strife, Egypt is a country which seems to be at peace with itself, at ease with its past.

No other nation on earth can claim such a glorious history as Egypt, and wherever the traveler wanders he will encounter, like Mahfouz's child, "the strange world of antiquities in all its immensity." When I first went to Egypt what struck me most about the great monuments of Pharaonic times was their vast scale: the Pyramids, the riverside temples, even the obelisks and statuary—everything seemed to render the buildings of today Lilliputian and shoddy. Lyons captures the grandeur of ancient Egypt quite brilliantly, yet the real strength of his photographs lies elsewhere: it is the images of neglect and decay which tell us most about contemporary attitudes toward the past, and by focusing on these Lyons explores the Egyptian psyche in the most subtle and revealing way. One of my favorite photographs in the book is of the step pyramid at Sakkara (p. 17): here time and the elements have worn away the hard edges of King Zoser's tomb, which has assumed an organic softness, like the desert itself. Look, too, at the *remarkable* photograph of two stone feet, severed at the ankle, standing in a weedy field near Thebes (p.59). As a surrealist image, it could scarcely be surpassed; but is this a photograph about the past, or the present? It is a measure of Lyons's skill that his photographs inspire inquiry as well as contemplation. More substantial than these trunkless feet, but no less tantalizing, are the ruins of the Ramesseum, where the broken colossus of Ramses II glows pink in the evening light. It was an etching of this scene which inspired Shelley's poem "Ozymandias":

> *And on the pedestal these words appear:*
> *"My name is Ozymandias, King of Kings:*
> *Look on my works, ye Mighty, and despair!"*

As a European one knows precisely what the poet means: when we dwell on the awesome nature of Egypt's past, how slight and ephemeral our own achievements seem! But such a point of view would strike most Egyptians as eccentric. It is not that they ignore or reject their prodigious history, with its ancient mosques, churches, pyramids and sarcophagi—"how they stirred my imagination and moved my sadness," writes Mahfouz; rather, they have come to terms with their past and learned to live with it. Indeed, until a century or so ago the great temples of Karnak, Luxor and elsewhere teemed with what one English lady described as "the sordid routine of Arab life." Here the peasantry would breed, trade, worship and die in shoulder-rubbing proximity to statues of gods and kings carved by their ancestors thousands of years before. None of this was appreciated by the tourists of Victorian times and the peasants were evicted from their temples. Nevertheless, Egyptians today still have their roots firmly anchored among these ancient ruins—metaphorically if not in fact.

Lyons has steered clear of the visual clichés to which so many photographers, on visiting Egypt, are unerringly attracted. This is not to say that he lacks an eye for drama— the opposite, in fact; it is just that he finds drama where others fail to see it. In some ways he reminds me of the French Impressionists of the last century: liberated from the artificial strictures of studio painting, they took their easels into the streets and fields and painted life as they found it. To them the hovel was as good a subject as the cathedral, and the peasant no less worthy of their attention than the well-to-do.

Robert Lyons is one of a long line of Western photographers to explore the visual possibilities of Egypt. Among the first was Maxime Du Camp, who traveled up the Nile in the company of Gustave Flaubert in 1850. As it happened, the latter's witty and perceptive journal proved rather more captivating than Du Camp's photographs. "This is indeed a funny country," declared Flaubert at one point. "Yesterday, for example, we were at a cafe which is one of the best in Cairo, and where there were, at the same time as ourselves, inside, a donkey shitting and a gentleman who was pissing in the corner. No one finds that odd." Yes, this is indeed a funny country, full of quirky contradictions, unexplained oddities and unbridled good humor. All of this comes across both in Mahfouz's story and in Lyons's photographs. One of the most memorable in this book depicts movie posters and apartment blocks reflected in the mirrors above a shop doorway (p. 47). The juxtaposition of art deco balcony—with upended armchair and a flat-dweller—with a couple kissing in the poster is astonishing. Lyons has also discovered humorous possibilities at a Coca-Cola stall (p. 85), and at a streetside bookstand (p. 24) where trashy romances share space with good novels and body-building magazines.

Lyons has a fine eye for color as well as composition. Egypt may lack the rich variety of brilliant colors one associates with places like Rajasthan and Senegal, but Lyons has captured those shades of blue, red and brown that I now think of as being peculiarly Egyptian. The turquoise-walled cafe in the Siwa Oasis (p. 49) is especially memorable, as are the bottles of pink and magenta pickle juice at the street stall in Qena (p. 45). And admire, too, the marvelous mosaic of ochers and umbers in the Western Desert near Giza (p. 21), and the serene blues of the Nile behind the more robust blue of a boatman's *jellabiah* (p. 93).

Lyons has the skills to draw the viewer into his photographs, and at times one feels not so much a voyeur as a participant. Take, for example, the photograph of the boatman mentioned above (p. 93): one has the illusion that one could take a few steps forward, shake hands and start a conversation. I get much the same feeling with the photograph of the manager at the Acropole Hotel in Alexandria (p. 23). All this makes for a rare sense of familiarity.

Though Lyons frequently captures the bizarre and incongruous, his work never seems contrived. He treats his subjects with sensitivity and humor, and browsing through his photographs I am constantly reminded of Mahfouz's assertion in "The Cradle": "There is so much to love . . ."

8 ■ SHARM AL-NAGA 1990

THE CRADLE

NAGUIB MAHFOUZ

As worries and anxieties cloud overhead, we are inclined to grope for love and warmth in the memories of things cherished in our hearts: tangible memories deep rooted in our existence. We may, in blazing heat, dry our sweat and quench our thirst with these. Joy is a tender hand and a tender embrace; a happy heedlessness of time; a Nile of passionate demands; wallowing in a garden of freedom without even knowing what it is; the delight of standing up, falling down, laughing; an arbitrary flood of solemn questions purely for fun; waiting for the squeal of the tram and the trolley on their slender rails to pierce the foliage; making small paper boats to launch in the little streams, to speed off from these tepid waters to undiscovered lands; whispering the heart's fondest hopes to saints' tombs; helping to stuff fish with hot spices, smearing them with batter.

In the still of the night, the call to dawn prayers is heard, and the heart pounds at the approach of morning and playtime. On the pillow lies the figure of a great traveler, made of painted tin; he asks him if he has voyaged to fairyland and seen wonders. There is so much to love: peddlers, boy scouts, circus parades, mobs of noisy boys, country relatives and their tales of ghosts and highwaymen (but every story has a happy ending).

Life's first love is of food, especially sweets. Home is full of milk pudding and heated rice pudding, milk, honey, molasses in tahini . . . and fruit! Watermelon, canteloupes and oranges, grapes, lotus fruit, peaches. The street is known for its doum fruit, candied apples, sugar-coated caraway seeds and gummy pistachio treats, pancakes, and at the top, chickpea candy and couscous. Sweets are so tempting in their meltingness, so bewitching in their aroma, so fast-acting upon the senses. They are the first exercise in the love of beauty. A child runs, grasping his tiny coins, never satisfied or jaded, to taste with keen craving everything good and delicious, crowning his campaign with knafeh, baklava, cake and chocolate.

A word or two teaches us the secret of this world and the next . . . we have so many troubles, and the darkness is imminent, but God is compassionate and merciful, bestowing His divine care and watching over everything. He gives us the key to security and peace in a verse we recite, in the prayers we perform, in the fasting that draws us near Him. The world turns sweet and serene, and blessings waft everywhere. Satan and his legions retreat. Paradise and its comforts await. Let us enhance our safety and peace by visiting a saint or hanging an amulet in our cap or burning a little incense.

"Happiness is not so hard to find, for those who want it."

■

An invitation to go out with Father and Mother is his heart's desire; he is proud in his sailor suit. His father sits with a group of friends in the Guindy Coffeehouse in Opera Square. He keeps to himself with a cup of ice cream, gazing at the square and the Ezbekiya Gardens, the statue of Ibrahim Pasha, intermittently following the men's conversation and listening gleefully to their laughter. Why do they laugh so loudly and twirl their mustaches? He does not know but his face shines at them and he laughs. He hears that So-and-so divorced his wife and that once al-Khaleeg Street was so flooded that it turned into a canal cutting Cairo in half. He asks his father:

"Like the love canal at the carnival?"

His father laughs.

"Ever since you discovered the carnival and the movies, you haven't been right in the head . . ." He shows the boy, in Ataba al-Khadra Square, a donkey stand as they head back to the old neighborhood. He suggests to his father that they ride donkeys home instead of taking the trolley, but his father groans.

"God help us, it's no use trying to civilize you!"

But he does not begrudge him buying a little easy-to-use machine for making ice cream and sherbet. He fills its inner compartment with buttermilk, or sometimes with lemonade, and at last gobbles up the ice cream or sherbet from the chamber.

■

The flat roof of the house is a kingdom whose whole area is blessed with total freedom, under the skies of all four seasons, in all their changing colors. A horizonscape of domes, of single and double minarets, frames the tower of al-Hussein, resembling a bride in its gorgeous, stirring stature. The little chicks huddle together in a knot under the railings as if it were a complete, colorful lush garden; the clucking of hens sounds from behind the wooden door. The rabbits' heads poke out of the slanted mouths of the earthenware jars. You gather up the eggs in the lap of your robe and offer clover stems to the rabbits. You toss feed to the chicks. There is an old cane chair which you enlist as your train, your tram, your car or jet; it becomes whatever you want with the speed of a longing imagination. This pail of water becomes a lake, the wooden ladder slumbering on the floor is transformed into a train track. Whim and dream and reality are all one. In the summer Mother moves the stove and clothes up to the roof, underneath the trellis of hyacinth. He joins in the new game if he pleases, washes the meat, pounds the spices in the mortar, peels the molokhiya. On holidays he helps decorate the cake, knead the dough or oil the sacrificial sheep.

On the roof, he sees a jet soar through space, its roar filling the sky, the tin mass of its toy fuselage gleaming. He sees the moon in the night and waits to watch for it on the Night of Power, to be blessed with luck and happiness. He watches the young back-alley women fighting like wild animals, and espies history, in the protest marches of militant men. He hears their cheers, and is a witness when their enemies pitilessly open fire upon them. There were wonderful nights, full of stars, when his mother spread out a fleece underneath the hyacinth and seated him there, in the light of a lantern blazing on top of a low table, to listen to tales of men and genies. Most of his time passes in solitude, but not in silence. He has unending dialogues with the chicks, the hens, the rabbits and the ants, and with inanimate things as well: the chair, the pail, the ladder, his tin toy. He goes even further, communicating with dreams and spirits. The roof is often a meeting place for family and neighbors, too; there are pleasant evening talk and soothing songs. Boys and girls play with one another, and with that little beauty, the daughter of the midwife, whose dark, subtle instincts led her to the perilous road of longing with wariness and elation.

One of the most festive holidays is the cemetery feast—isn't it the feast of flowers, pancakes and sweet basil? And the trip, with his parents, in a parade of men, women and children? The gates of the courtyard open to you; the entry is sprinkled with sand and water. There are baskets in the alms room, and we all hurry to cover the tomb with flowers . . . it awaits the visitors unchanged, immersed in silence and mystery, provoking wonder and curiosity. He peeks from its pedestal to see if what is inside will come out of the opening. He sees no ancestors or relatives resting peacefully, enjoying relief and intimacy from the recitations of this visit. His parents address the tomb with strange speech, as if addressing living people able to listen and answer. They are reciting the Koran and handing out alms to the poor and beggars. He tiptoes outside and finds himself among playmates, absorbed in storytelling. Everything makes him so happy. Why are his eyes filling with tears?

What's with this neighbor who sometimes appears on her roof, the one beside ours?

She's watering plants or feeding the pigeons. She has radiant white skin, and her black hair down in a long, loose braid. Her gaze is sweet and cheerful, her manner light and alluring. She is much older than he is, but his mother talks to her as she would to any daughter of her own. He enjoys her company and speaks to her nicely, and sometimes she brings him halva bars with sesame seed. When she visited his mother, with her mother, she lifted him up with both hands and kissed him. He feels embarrassed with her, but wants more of her. When he has nothing to do, she occupies his mind. Once, his mother spoke to him about it in front of his father.

"You stare at that girl all the time—do you want to eat her?"

"What do you want from her?" asked his father.

He was a little startled.

"I want to marry her!"

His father laughed.

"Oh, God. Wait until you can spell your name right!"

The heart craves Ramadan and the two great feasts, and counts the days until their arrival. It is from the pantry that we first learn of the approach of the fasting month: its walls are crammed with packages of dried fruits. He yearns to fast, but his mother refuses to wake him for suhhour, the last meal before daybreak. She lets him fast for the few hours he can, and habituates him slowly until the fast truly starts punishing him at seven o'clock and again at prayertime. His mother mitigated her fast with uncounted delights. The suhhour, the iftar, the lanterns, the toys between the square and al-Hussein; humming songs. In the last days of the month, his father takes him to New Street, to Jaquelle & Gustar, and buys him a new suit and new shoes. He saves them for the morning of the feast day, examining them lovingly, smelling with epicurean passion the aroma of new leather and cloth. He was given a bath and haircut, dressed in all his finery, and they set off to the scene of celebrations, of flutes and swings and seesaws. Cake, pastry, gifts, visits to relatives and dear friends, the Egyptian Club Cinema, Charlie Chaplin and Mashist. On Eid al-Adha, he experiences new friendship with the sheep, and betrayal, at dawn of the promised day. For iftar he has grilled meat, for lunch bread stew and waffles. In those days, love for God moved the young heart no less than love for beautiful neighbors, candy and pistachio brittle.

Sensual bliss goes beyond food and sweets. Greenery peeps out from the hyacinth trellis and the flowerpots of carnations. The trolley makes its way in the flowery fields of al-Qubba, driven by its barefoot conductor. The greenery and flowers make the heart quiver with bounding joy and wonderful secret conversations; the little streams whip up the memory of the soul. He has known their seductive smells since the distilling of flower and rose water from the water tank in the bath of the old house . . . And audible bliss? It is in the speeches made at weddings and the lovely phonograph evenings when they listened to the recitations of readers, popular songs from all over the world, the songs of Abdelhai Hilmi, al-Manilawi, Saleh, Munira, al-Banna and Sayid Darwish, then Umm Kalthoum, and Abdelwahab—each individual delightful sound offers a haven in which to linger and relax.

When and how did the Egyptian Club Cinema steal my heart? How did its tales of the American West join my roll call of love and loved things, along with the comedy of Charlie Chaplin, the strength of Mashist, the beauty of Mary Pickford? At first I thought the magic and dream were real, in a place somewhere behind the screen, in Khan Gaafar or Watawit Alley. I eventually conceded that they were just pictures, only representing true facts, not made-up stories. I longed to spend my whole life in front of the screen, with the characters, and loved Mary Pickford, and treasured the imagined resemblance between her and my pretty neighbor. I fervently believed that William S. Hart's real name was Ali al-Dayan and that he came from Shaariya Gate; that he might appear to me on a tiny hand-cranked viewer, lit by a gas lamp, equipped with short strips chopped from the movie reels unbeknownst to the owners, which I would run in the little rooftop room, which, thanks to the viewer, would become a refuge for the little girls of the neighborhood.

Acting out stirring scenes is another delight . . . My father was the first person I ever mimicked, and my mother too; and a short time before that it ended in my getting punished. Imitating our religious teacher with his cloth switch around my head like a turban, I squatted on a box with the janitor sitting in front of me while I imitated his voice and brandished a pointer. I read the lesson, listened and meted out punishment, getting revenge on all those who used to chase me. I covered the box with a sheet to turn it into a tomb. I addressed it just as my parents addressed the tomb: "Peace be with you, Father; peace be with you, Mother." And I recited some prayers. My mother got very angry at that and rained blows on me. I imitated the tough boys at play, waving the stick in the air, and the demonstrators who chanted "Long Live Saad!" and "Down with Protectionism!" I imitated the peddlers, the crowds and some of the rather intriguing women, and at times even the overloaded camels whose braying assaulted my ears from the square, and I would then be assailed by either exasperation or admiration, depending on the day and the circumstances.

The happy visits to the homes of my brothers and sisters lifted us out of the old neighborhood into new ones such as al-Hadayiq, Sakakini and al-Zahira . . . I rush into the house to find a strange man, and in the other an unknown woman, but we all exchange embraces of love and welcome; there, the newborn babies lie in the cradle or cuddle against grownups. Compared to them I'm a fully grown man, and we kiss and play with baby toys under the strictest adult surveillance. There are degrees of love from house to house; one house seems to me an extension of my own, with its warmth and familiarity, the other has a certain reserve which only I seem to sense. Still, in general, it is a close, loyal and loving family, and I have no memory of a single thorn sprouting from its lush greenery. How much I loved them! How much they loved me!

I appreciated the strange world of antiquities in all its immensity before I ever set foot in school. When I revisited it on school trips, it was a return to a wonderland whose emblems were etched into my heart and imagination forever. My first step was with my father; then my mother fell under the spell, and it became one of her rituals. The sarcophagi, the ancient mosques, the churches and Sufi monasteries, the Pyramids, the Pharaonic, Islamic and Coptic antiquity museums, how they stirred my imagination and moved my sadness! My father's commentary was very clipped—but my mother, where did she ever get all those stories from? We spent the longest time in the Mummy Room.

She leans over the sarcophagus, looking sad and rather humble.

"Are they alive?" I ask her.

"They've been dead for a long time."

"Are our relatives in the tomb like them now?"

She gives me a serious answer: "God alone knows how they are."

"Will we all have to die?" I ask her earnestly.

"After a long, long life, God willing," she smiles.

This answer reassures me.

Friendship is one of life's greatest blessings. A friend was always there on the roof, in the square, in the alley, transient and resident, and relatives passing through and staying with us, if they were some of our country cousins. We played indoors and outside. I was their guide through the al-Hussein neighborhood; they walked behind me like tourists, munching fruit. From Beit al-Qadi to Khan Gaafar to al-Hussein and New Street, Ghouria, Sinaa, Nahasin, Watawit, Qormuz, Kababgi, Palace Walk, the Syrian Quarter, Qasr al-Shawq, Sukkaria; we gaped at the lunatics at the Bab al-Akhdar. The houseguests often went out, more gracefully and peaceably, walking or jogging behind the water-sprinkling wagons, telling stories or singing group songs; most elegant among them were the eye doctor, Sheikh Beshir, and al-Efatenti. No outing was without an encounter with street boys, who, despite their ragged clothes and bare feet, could be uproarious and charming; and their contempt for convention was boundless. They sang scandalous songs, which we knew instinctively would condemn whoever learned them to worldly misery and ever-lasting hellfire, but a day without seeing those boys or hearing their songs was utterly unthinkable.

A fleeting period; in a dreamer's eyes, the first step on an endless road. A mere preliminary step, followed by school and boyhood, youth, adulthood and old age. Life in all its orderly dimensions.

But slowly:

A short period, but bearing unnumbered embryonic possibilities. It bears witness to eternal questions, to love, sex, friendship, honor, life, death, the glorious Presence of the Almighty, basic themes that develop and diversify with life, taking from the rich sea rushing waves and vast horizons. These still scatter to us longings and meditations, dreams and deeds, self-absorption and exuberance, never relinquishing our everlasting wish to discover the lamp that will light the path of fate.

17 ■ PYRAMID ZOSER, SAKKARA 1981

19 ■ KARNAK VILLAGE, LUXOR 1981

21 ■ WESTERN DESERT FROM GIZA PLATEAU 1981

25 ■ AL-HOURIA DISTRICT, CAIRO 1985

26 ■ MIDAN TALAAT HARB, CAIRO 1990

28 ■ AL-SAIDA ZEINAB, CAIRO 1991

29 ■ CAMEL MARKET, IMBABA 1991

33 ■ MOSQUE OF AL-MARDANI, CAIRO 1991

35 ■ WINDOW, CAIRO 1989

36 ■ PILGRIM'S HOTEL, KHAN AL-KHALILI 1989

38 ■ LABORER, CAIRO 1989

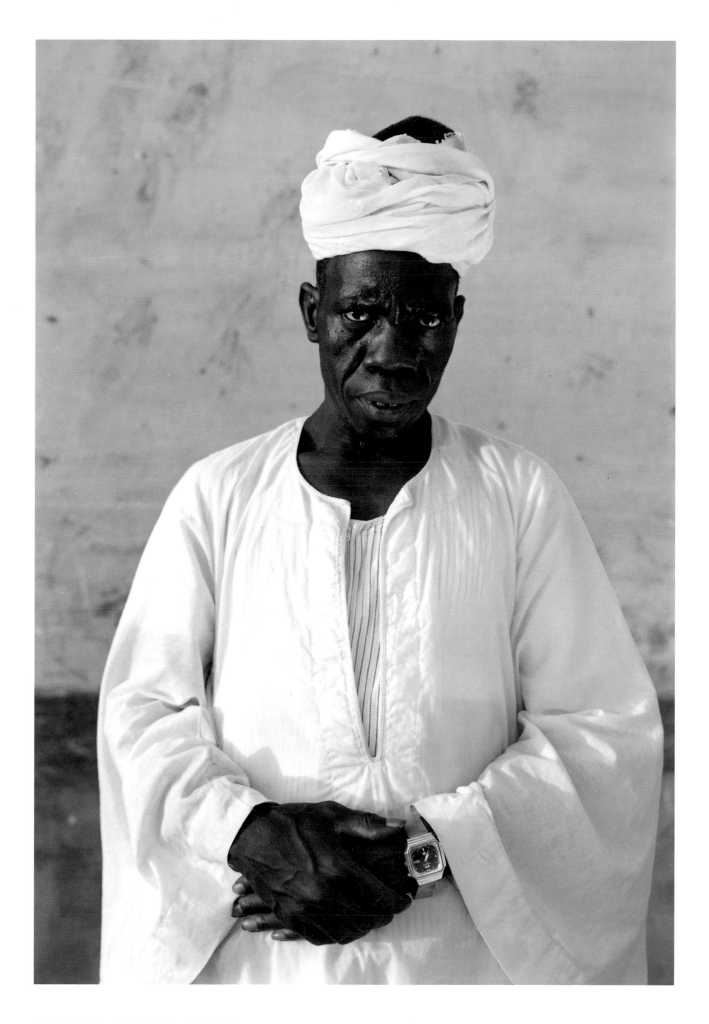

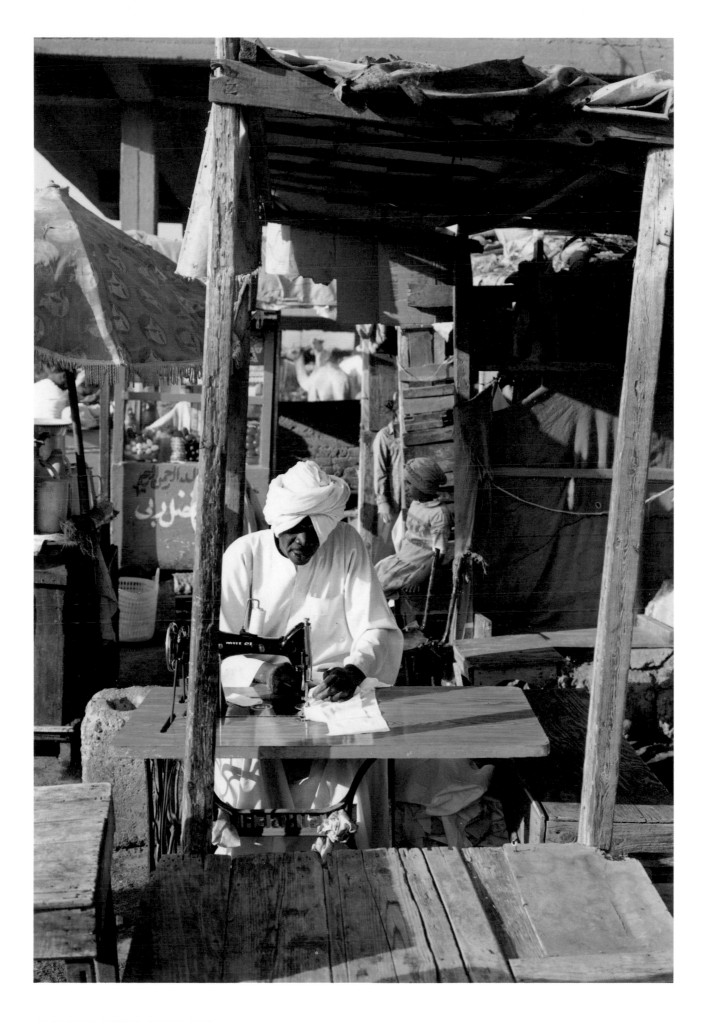

41 ■ CAMEL MARKET, IMBABA 1991

45 ■ FOUL AND FALAFEL STAND, QENA 1985

49 ■ BLUE ROOM, SIWA OASIS 1989

51 ■ CAFE, SIWA OASIS 1989

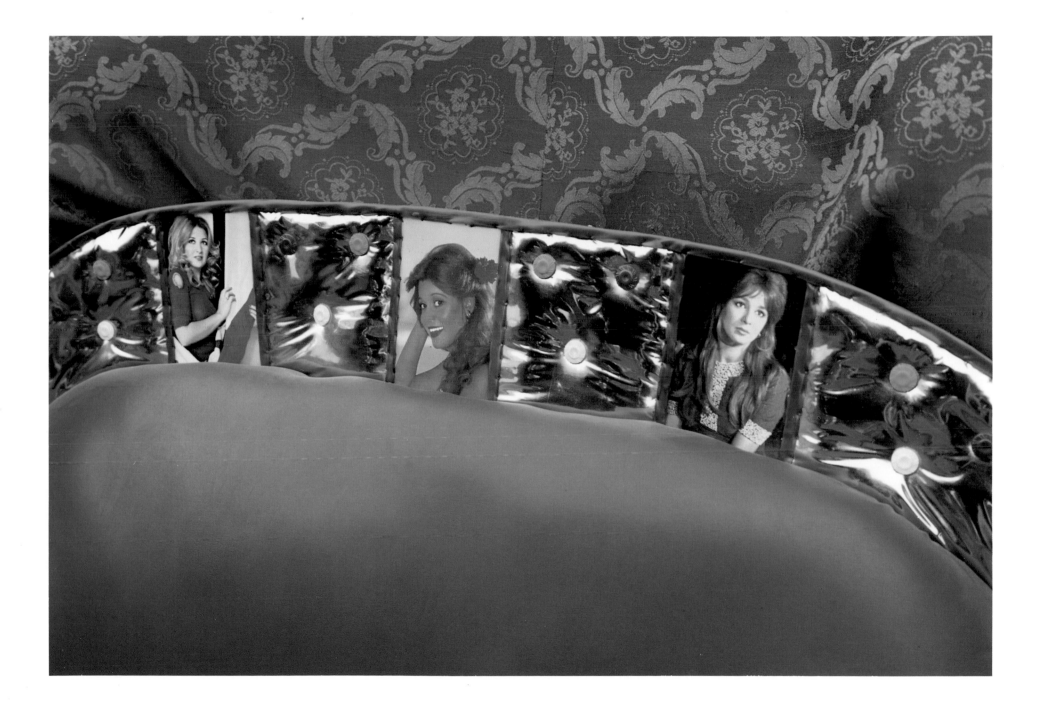

55 ■ DELTA, NEAR MANSURA 1985

57 ■ POMPEY'S PILLAR, ALEXANDRIA 1989

61 ■ TOMB, CITY OF THE DEAD 1985

63 ■ QAIT BEY FORT, ALEXANDRIA 1989

64 ■ MIAMEY BEACH, ALEXANDRIA 1991

66 ■ MONESTERLY PALACE, RODA ISLAND 1981

69 ■ SPICE MERCHANT, KHAN AL-KHALILI 1985

71 ■ CAFE, CAIRO 1981

75 ■ METALSMITH, CITY OF THE DEAD 1990

77 ■ NILE, CAIRO 1981

81 ■ KASR AL-NIL BRIDGE, CAIRO 1989

84 ■ CINEMA MIAMEY, CAIRO 1990

88 ■ MIDAN SAAD ZAGHOUL, ALEXANDRIA 1990

89 ■ FERRYBOAT, LUXOR 1989

93 ■ SAILMAKERS, LUXOR 1981

95 ■ WOMEN CARRYING WATER, THEBES 1981

97 ■ MOSQUE OF AMIR AQSUNQUR, CAIRO 1989

AFTERWORD

ROBERT LYONS

We were glad to have seen the land which was the mother of civilization, which taught Greece her letters and through Greece, Rome, and through Rome the world; that land which knew three thousand years ago, well-nigh all of medicine and surgery which science has *discovered* lately; . . . which had in high excellence a thousand luxuries and necessities of an advanced civilization which we have gradually contrived and accumulated in modern times and claimed as things that were new under the sun; . . . that old land that knew all we know now, perchance and more; that walked in the broad highway of civilization in the gray dawn of creation, ages and ages before we were born.

MARK TWAIN
from *The Innocents Abroad*

I first discovered Egypt through its antiquities that John Lowell brought back in 1834. As a child I was often taken to the Boston Museum of Fine Arts to see the hieroglyphs, scepters of gold, sarcophagi and mummies. It was the mummies in particular that intrigued me. What did these people look like? How did they live? What language did they speak? I was filled with questions.

I did not have an opportunity to travel to Egypt until 1981. Following in the footsteps of such men of renown as Napoleon, Melville, Du Camp, Flaubert, Frith and Gustave LeGray, I was first enraptured with the romance of Egypt. Over time I became truly enamored with its people and distinctive landscape. This landscape derives its uniqueness from a variety of factors: its aridness, historical monuments and the sheer vastness of the desert, with the Nile cutting a rich green swath down its center. Indeed the enormity of the monuments and their numbers in the land are a constant reminder of Egypt's past glories and its importance in the Western mind. Often in the light of the midday sun the terrain can seem daunting, especially on the edge of the desert. But as the crepuscular time of day approaches, the astounding beauty of the place and its history are revealed. Here, perhaps more than anywhere else, everything depends upon light, that great magician who in a second can transform the trivial into the extraordinary.

It was coincidence that led me to meet Naguib Mahfouz. I had been reading modern Arabic writers, at least those who had been translated into English, since the early 1980s. On my first trip to Cairo I stumbled upon the bookstore at the American University in Cairo, which had a large selection of translated books by Arabic writers. There I discovered *Midaq Alley* by Mahfouz. I devoured it as I walked the very streets he had written about. When, sadly, I finished the book I happened to be at Fishawi's Cafe. Fishawi's is one of the oldest cafes in the Khan al-Khalili and it was a favorite of Mahfouz's in his younger days. Tucked away in a long alley near the Hussein Mosque, its interior is lined with fancy woodwork (mashabriya), mirrors and chandeliers covered with Islamic designs. Still a gathering place for writers, musicians and families, I felt that the characters from the book were right there around me.

I continued to read Mahfouz's books and in 1989 I was fortunate enough to meet him. It was November and I had just arrived in Egypt a few days earlier. On my flight from New York City to Cairo, somewhere over the middle of the Atlantic, I opened a magazine randomly—the headline read "Mahfouz at the Ali Baba." By coincidence or fate I had the means to find Mahfouz in a city of fifteen million people. My first mornings were spent in search of the Ali Baba Cafe.

I had heard that Mahfouz woke early each day and walked to the Ali Baba. I set off at 6:45 A.M. Cairo was gray, murky and overcast, looking like what I imagine Eastern Europe to be. The clouds dampened the din of the automobiles and the sounds of the muezzins' call to prayer lent an odd eeriness to the scene.

Climbing the stairs to the second floor of the Ali Baba, I saw an old man peering out the window at the waking city. The room Mahfouz sits in every morning is lined with cedarwood and lit with small wall sconces. It feels very warm in contrast with the damp, cool morning. A single chair and table are set out in the center of the room for its sole occupant. Mahfouz faced out and did not seem to encourage contact. Beside him was a stack of daily newspapers and on the table his cup of Turkish coffee. Working up my courage, I passed through a glass door and entered the room. I walked directly up to the table before Mr. Mahfouz realized my presence. *"Ahalan wasahlan,"* he said, greeting me in Arabic. I returned the greeting, he smiled and put out his hand. Since that initial meeting we have met often on my subsequent visits.

The photographs in this book were taken on various trips to Egypt over the past ten years. I usually spent a block of time, four weeks or more, exploring specific areas and ideas. For most of the pictures I worked with a medium-format camera with a fixed-focal-length lens. Occasionally I shot with a 35mm camera. The use of a very wide or very long lens seems to me to place method before meaning, often causing an essential charm of a photograph to be lost. This charm is the photograph's gradual revelation of its essence after long examination. All the pictures were done on color negative film from which I made color prints. For me this process allows the most control over color, hue and visual nuance.

ACKNOWLEDG- MENTS

ROBERT LYONS

I wish to thank the many individuals who made me feel at home during my visits to Egypt and allowed me to embrace it as my own for a brief time. The following people in particular I thank for their generous assistance and advice while in Egypt: Madame Rawia al-Monesterly of the Egyptian Press Office, Barry Iverson, Susan Lezan, and Raymond Stock. I especially thank Hassan Ragab, Tewfik Hassan Mohammed, Rifat al-Sayed and Mohammed Fathy al-Sayed of Cairo, who assisted at various stages and have become my extended family.

For their continuing belief and support in my work and in this project I thank Bill Arnold, Mitch Epstein, Joseph Defazio, Jerome Leibling, Christina Roessler, Elaine Mayes, Sheron Rupp and Isaiah Wyner.

I especially wish to thank Marit Nieuwland for her support and enthusiasm throughout the production of the book, and her assistance in Egypt and the United States.

I thank Mr. Ric Immediatio, Director of Sales for Gulf Air in the United States and Canada.

I thank the American University in Cairo Press for their permission to use Mr. Mahfouz's story and in particular Ms. Aleya Serour for her assistance.

For his spirit of adventure and his sensitive response to the photographs and story I thank Charlie Pye-Smith.

Peter Theroux enthusiastically embraced the project and provided the excellent translation of the story—thank you.

I want to especially thank Naguib Mahfouz for his encouragement and friendship. His wonderful gift of the story which accompanies the photographs allows extended insight into them.

Throughout the production of the book a number of people have helped. I wish to thank: Jeffrey Johnston, Cynthia Shyvers, the staff at Doubleday and in particular Katy Homans who designed the book.

Finally, for their belief in this project and their support throughout, I wish to thank my editors at Doubleday — Jacqueline Onassis and Shaye Areheart.

ROBERT LYONS